MOUNT ROYAL SCHOOL LIBRARY.

DISCOVERING
MEXICO

By Marion Morrison

A ZOË BOOK

MOUNT ROYAL SCHOOL LIBRARY

A ZOË BOOK

© 1996 Zoë Books Limited

Devised and produced by
Zoë Books Limited
15 Worthy Lane
Winchester
Hampshire SO23 7AB
England

Apart from any fair dealing for the purposes of research or private study, or criticism or review, as permitted under the Copyright, Designs and Patents Act, 1988, this publication may only be reproduced, stored or transmitted, in any form or by any means, with the prior permission in writing of the publishers, or in the case of reprographic reproduction in accordance with the terms of licences issued by the Copyright Licensing Agency.

Any person who does any unauthorised act in relation to this publication may be liable to criminal prosecution and civil claims for damages.

First published in Great Britain in 1996 by
Zoë Books Limited
15 Worthy Lane
Winchester
Hampshire SO23 7AB

A record of the CIP data is available from the British Library.

ISBN 1 874488 60 6

Printed in Italy by Grafedit SpA
Design: Jan Sterling, Sterling Associates
Map: Gecko Limited
Production: Grahame Griffiths

Photographic acknowledgments
The publishers wish to acknowledge, with thanks, the following photographic sources:

South American Pictures / Tony Morrison – Cover, 5, 6, 7, 9, 10, 11, 12, 13, 14, 15, 16, 17t, 18, 19, 20, 21, 22, 23, 24, 27, 28, 29; / Robert Francis – title page, 8, 17b; / Chris Sharp 25b; Zefa 25t; / A. Photri 26.

The publishers have made every effort to trace the copyright holders, but if they have inadvertently overlooked any, they will be pleased to make the necessary arrangement at the first opportunity.

917.2 Oct 96 13,115
MOR

Cover: *The Maya pyramid of the Soothsayer, Uxmal*

Title page: *Heavy traffic on the main avenue leading to The Monument to the Revolution in the centre of Mexico City*

Contents

¡Bienvenido!	5
Mountains and plains	6
Blue seas, hot sand	8
Ancient civilisations	10
Conquest and revolutions	12
Peoples of Mexico	14
Mexico City	16
Tortillas and beans	18
Having fun	20
The world of the arts	22
Working the land	24
Energy and industry	26
Modern Mexico	28
Fact file	30
Index	32

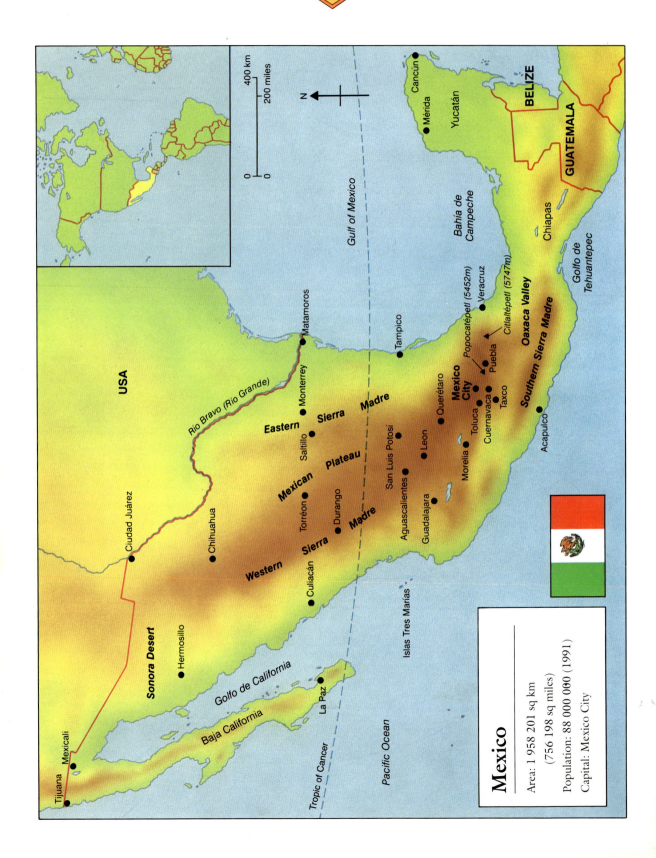

¡Bienvenido!

Welcome to Mexico! Its full name in Spanish is *Los Estados Unidos Mexicanos*, which means the United Mexican States. This is the vast country that lies between the USA and the lands of Central and South America.

Its northern border with the USA is almost 3000 kilometres (over 1860 miles) long. Much of it follows the famous Río Grande, a river known in Mexico as the Río Bravo. In the south Mexico shares frontiers with Guatemala and tiny Belize, once a British colony. To the east it faces the Gulf of Mexico and the Caribbean Sea, and to the west the Pacific Ocean.

A family in Uruapan market

Ninety-one steps lead to the top of the Pyramid of Kukulcan. This was the most important building in Chichén Itzá, the ancient city of the Maya and Toltecs.

Mexico is a country of great contrasts. It has snow-capped mountains and volcanoes, tropical forests, fertile valleys and plains, barren deserts and white-sand beaches. Almost 20 million people live in the capital, Mexico City. The people of Mexico are mainly of Spanish and Native American descent.

A rich heritage

Mexico is perhaps most famous for its ancient civilisations. The Maya, Toltec and Aztec peoples inhabited the country long before the Spaniards arrived in the sixteenth century. They built huge stone temples, palaces and pyramids, which are visited by thousands of tourists every year. Mexico also has many fine churches, built during the 300 years of Spanish rule. Some churches have magnificent carvings and are lavishly decorated with gold and silver.

Mountains and plains

More than half of Mexico lies over 1000 metres (3280 feet) above sea level. The two main highland regions are the west and east ranges of the Sierra Madre mountains. Some very deep canyons cut into the western range. The most spectacular is the 'Copper Canyon', which is often compared to the Grand Canyon of the USA. The eastern range is the higher of the two, with peaks of over 3657 metres (12 000 feet).

Between the two ranges is a plain, known as the Mexican Plateau, which extends from the United States border to south of Mexico City. The northern part of the plateau is dry and difficult to farm. Not many people live there. By contrast, the southern part, which is about 2450 metres (over 8000 feet) above sea level, has fertile valleys. Many of the main cities, such as Puebla, Guadalajara and Mexico City itself, are located here. This region represents only 14 per cent of Mexico, but it is home to almost half the population.

Southern highlands

The rugged southern Sierra Madre mountains line the Pacific coast. Their forested slopes provide a spectacular backdrop to the country's best known tourist resort, Acapulco. In these mountains there are plateaux and valleys. The Oaxaca valley is home to some of Mexico's poorest farmers.

In the far south the forest-covered Chiapas highlands are inhabited mainly by the Maya, a Native American people who live in remote, isolated villages.

The main square, Guadalajara

The Popocatépetl volcano

Volcanoes

A line of spectacular snow-capped volcanoes crosses the southern edge of the Mexican Plateau. On a fine day, the summits of two can be seen from Mexico City. Their Native American names, Iztaccíhuatl and Popocatépetl, mean 'the sleeping woman' and 'the smoking mountain'. Mexico's highest volcano is Citlaltépetl, also called Orizaba, which is in the eastern Sierra Madre and is 5747 metres (18 854 feet) high.

Buried in lava

The Paricutín volcano first erupted on 20 February 1943. Rocks, smoke and fire burst out of the ground, eventually reaching a height of 1300 metres (4265 feet). The volcano remained active for 11 years, and buried the nearby village of San Juan. As the lava cooled, all that could be seen was the top of the old village church.

Hot – and cold

Although the southern half of Mexico is in the tropics, the climate depends mainly on the height of the land. The levels up to 750 metres (over 2460 feet) are known as the hot land, or *tierra caliente*. The mild or temperate zone (*tierra templada*) lies between 750 and 2000 metres (2460 and 6562 feet). Higher still is the cold land or *tierra fría*.

The coastal regions are generally hot, the plateaux temperate and the mountains cold. It can actually be quite warm in the mountains during the day, but it can be bitterly cold at night. Winter is said to be a dry season and summer a rainy season. But Mexico suffers from a general lack of rain and there are really only two areas where it rains all year round.

The Paricutín volcano

Blue seas, hot sand

A beach in the Yucatán

Mexico has over 10 000 kilometres (6250 miles) of coastline. The coast facing the Gulf of Mexico is 1500 kilometres (over 900 miles) long and runs from the US border to the Yucatán peninsula. The Gulf coast scenery changes as you travel south, from the dry lands of the north through a central region of swamps and lagoons, to dense, tropical rainforest in the south. Veracruz, Mexico's main port, is on this coast.

A tropical paradise

The Yucatán peninsula is the most easterly point of Mexico. It has long, white sandy beaches lined with tropical palms. The green-blue waters of the Caribbean Sea are ideal for many water sports. Offshore there are islands such as Cozumel, famous for its coral reefs. Here there are amazing shoals of brightly coloured tropical fish.

Inland most of the peninsula is covered by scrub and forest, but this is where many of the greatest Maya pyramids can be found. It is not surprising that the Yucatán has become the most important tourist area in Mexico. New resorts, like Cancún, have been built with luxurious skyscraper hotels to accommodate the increasing number of wealthy tourists from overseas.

A water pipeline in the Sonora desert

Northwestern deserts

The northwest corner of Mexico has the sort of scenery you see in cowboy films. It is the land of the Sonora and Great Mexican Deserts. There are a few towns, but mostly it is just burning sand, cacti, dunes and rocks, stretching out to the horizon on every side. Only further south, where rivers cross the narrow Pacific lowlands, is it possible to farm and raise cattle.

Baja California

The Baja California peninsula is 1300 km (over 800 miles) long and seldom over 165 km (over 100 miles) wide. Despite its long coastline, the inland region is arid and mountainous.

Few people live outside the main towns of Tijuana and Mexicali on the US border, and La Paz in the south.

Monkeys, snakes and whales

Mexico's rainforests are home to noisy monkeys, fierce jaguars and long-snouted anteaters. The forest's heaviest mammal is the tapir, a distant relative of the rhinoceros. There are all sorts of colourful tropical birds such as parrots and macaws.

Surprisingly there is also animal life in the deserts, where small rodents, rabbits, snakes and lizards have adapted to the arid conditions. The tropical oceans teem with marine life. Grey whales, at one time in danger of extinction, winter in the warm waters of Baja California.

There are many national parks in Mexico, but in places the wildlife is threatened by the destruction of the forest for farming and grazing.

A jaguar in the rainforest

Ancient civilisations

The Palace at Palenque. The tower was probably used as an observatory.

Early peoples survived in the Americas by hunting, gathering fruit and nuts, and by fishing. In time they learned to grow basic crops like maize. They gradually began to settle in small groups, often close to rivers.

By 1200BC the first major civilisation had grown up on the Gulf coast. The Olmec people carved colossal stone heads and beautiful jade figures, often of jaguars. In about 400BC the Zapotecs founded their city at Monte Albán, from which they controlled the Oaxaca valley for about 800 years.

Carvings and calendars

The ancient civilisation best known to us today was that of the Maya. Their lands stretched from the Yucatán into Central America. They were at their greatest between AD300 and 800. Skilled scientists and astronomers, they worked out an accurate 365-day calendar long before one was used in Europe. They had a form of writing using small pictures or 'glyphs'. These were carved on stone to record Mayan history.

The ancient Maya were also great architects and are famous for their stone-built cities such as Chichén Iztá and Palenque. Deep in the Temple of the Inscriptions at Palenque lies the tomb of the great Mayan ruler Pacal, who came to power in AD615 at the age of only 12.

Glyphs and carvings in the Temple tell the story of Pacal's long life until he died at the age of 80.

> **'The city of the gods'**
> Teotihuacán, in the Valley of Mexico, was the greatest of all the ancient cities. No one is sure who built it or who lived there. It probably dates from AD300 to AD600 and its rich palaces, temples and pyramids were built on a rectangular, grid pattern. It formed a city large enough for perhaps 200 000 people.

Toltec warriors

Other civilisations included the Toltecs, a fierce and warlike people who ruled much of the centre of Mexico by force in the eleventh and twelfth centuries. Their centre was at Tula, where today a group of stone warrior-like figures still stand on the skyline.

The Aztec empire

The Aztecs were the last of the great Native American civilisations in Mexico. At the time when the Spaniards invaded the region in 1519, the Aztec ruler Montezuma II controlled an empire of about 10 million people. Aztec society was very well organised. The capital, Tenochtitlán, had been built for legendary reasons on islands in Lake Texcoco. It became a wealthy and powerful city which amazed the Spaniards. Crops were grown on *chinampas*, floating gardens in the lake. There were bustling markets, and many temples and pyramids.

Toltec figures at Tula

Ruins of the Great Aztec Temple in Mexico City

Conquest and revolutions

Some of the first Spanish explorers to reach the Americas thought they had reached Asia. They called the local, or indigenous, peoples 'Indians'.

It was a Spanish conqueror called Hernán Cortés who reached the Gulf coast in 1519. Within two years he had defeated the Aztecs and made Mexico a Spanish colony called New Spain.

The Europeans set out to find riches and to convert the people to Christianity. Huge amounts of silver and gold were sent back to Spain. The Mexicans suffered badly. They were forced to work in the mines and on the land. Millions died from diseases such as smallpox and influenza, which were brought in by the Europeans.

The new republic

The first call for independence from Spain was made by a priest called Miguel Hidalgo in the town of Dolores, on 15 September 1810. This *Grito de Dolores* – 'the cry from Dolores' – is now seen to have been a turning point in Mexican history. It took 11 years and the lives of half a million Mexicans before the struggle was won in 1821.

The next 40 years were chaotic. The country had huge debts, there were civil wars and no fewer than 56 changes of government. The most powerful man was the dictator General López de Santa

This mural of Independence was painted by Juan O'Gorman in 1960-61.

Anna. Change only came when he was overthrown in 1855.

> ### A country halved
> Santa Anna was not a good ruler. In 1846 Mexico lost a war with the USA. By 1848, Mexico had lost half its territory – including the lands of Texas and California – to the USA.

Rebels and dictators

One of Mexico's great heroes was one of the Zapotec people. He was called Benito Juárez and was president from 1857-64 and 1867-72. He wanted to reduce the power of the Church, which was very wealthy but which did little to help the ordinary people.

A statue of Benito Juárez, Mexico City

Porfirio Díaz was a very different leader. He was a dictator who took power in 1876 and kept it for 34 years. He improved the country's economy but under his rule the poor lacked even basic rights. All the land and wealth were owned by about 20 per cent of the population. The needs of the poor and demands for land reform led to a stormy revolution.

Díaz was overthrown. Various sections of Mexican society took up the slogan '*Tierra y Libertad*' – 'land and freedom'. The Mexican Revolution was under way. Emiliano Zapata and Pancho Villa were the heroes of the ordinary people. Both were assassinated, but eventually the struggle was won. Reforms began when Lázaro Cárdenas became president in 1934. One of his first actions was to break up the large estates and re-distribute the land.

Emiliano Zapata

Peoples of Mexico

People gather to celebrate the festival of the Virgin of Guadalupe in Mexico City.

Over the ages, Mexico's Spanish invaders mixed with local indigenous peoples. Today about 60 per cent of Mexicans are *mestizos*, people of mixed descent. Spanish is the official language.

In the towns and cities *mestizos* wear similar clothes to people in Europe or the USA. In some country areas village women wear blouses, long skirts and shawls called *rebozos*. They use these to cover their heads and also, sometimes, for carrying babies. Men wear cotton shirts and trousers and leather sandals called *huaraches*. They always have a wide-brimmed hat or *sombrero*, to protect them against the sun. Often men carry a poncho or a colourful blanket called a *serape*, for protection against the rain or a cold night.

Home life

Family life is very important to Mexicans. The average household has five or six people, as well as an extended family of aunts, uncles, cousins and friends. By tradition, the man is the head of the household and the woman does the housework and brings up the children. However, times are changing and more young women now go out to work and have careers.

A young girl's First Communion

Candles and processions

Mexico has no official state religion, but over 90 per cent of the people are Roman Catholics. Christenings, First Communions and weddings are all important occasions in family life, usually celebrated with a large party.

Families also enjoy the many festivals and pageants that celebrate holy days. One important festival is the Day of the Dead, when masses of flowers, candles, special breads, sweets shaped into skulls and other foods are placed in homes and on graves to remember the dead.

Indigenous peoples

There are over 50 groups of Native American peoples in Mexico, each with their own language or dialect. Two of the larger groups are the Maya of the Yucatán and Chiapas regions, and the Zapotec of the Oaxaca valley. Others, like the Lacandones, number just a few dozen families.

Many of the indigenous peoples live like country *mestizos*, growing the food they need and making a living selling produce and crafts in local markets. Even the long-haired Tarahumaras of the Sonora Desert survive in this way.

Others lead a more difficult life. In remote villages there are no modern facilities like running water or electricity. The Huichols in the Sierra Madre mountains are known to prefer to live this way.

Most of the indigenous peoples still wear their distinctive dress, and keep up their traditional festivals and ceremonies. But change may be on the way. Most of them do not own any land, and recently the Maya of Chiapas have been threatening to take violent action unless something is done.

Weaving cloth in a market

Mexico City

Founded in 1521, Mexico City was built by the Spaniards on the remains of the Aztec capital, Tenochtitlán. It is 2240 metres (almost 7500 feet) above sea level. This vast city now contains a quarter of Mexico's population.

The capital is the centre of the country's political, commercial and cultural life. It is a city of great contrasts, with colonial and nineteenth century architecture alongside modern buildings of steel and glass. Some people live in great wealth in well-planned residential areas, while others experience extreme poverty in shanty towns.

The hub of the city is the Zócalo, or main square, and around it stand many fine colonial buildings. Wide tree-lined boulevards cross the city, passing by shopping precincts and parks. Mexico city is noisy, bustling and lived-in. If you cannot find what you want in one of the countless markets or craft shops, try the street-sellers who line the pavements and the main squares. If you want a letter typed, drop into Printer's Square, where any one of a row of men with very old typewriters will do it for you.

Earthquake tragedy

About 10 000 people are believed to have died in an earthquake that hit Mexico City in 1985. Two hundred modern high-rise buildings were damaged or destroyed and some 300 000 people left homeless.

A view from central Mexico City looking north

The cathedral and the Zócalo

Sights to see

The National Palace – This was built in 1692 on the site of Montezuma's ancient palace.
The Cathedral – The largest – and oldest – in all Latin America.
Chapultepec Palace and **Park** – former home of Emperor Maximilian.
Latin American Tower – From the 41st floor there is a magnificent view of the city.
The University City – The modern university has a spectacular mosaic of the history of Mexican culture.
Palace of Fine Arts – There are regular art exhibitions by Mexico's greatest painters.
Museum of Anthropology and Archaeology – This is one of the finest museums in the world.
Templo Mayor – The Great Aztec Temple of Tenochtitlán was found in 1978 and is now being excavated.

City of problems

Mexico City has many problems. By the year 2000 its population is expected to reach more than 25 million, and it is likely to be the largest city in the world. Thousands of people arrive each day from poor country areas. The newcomers have to live in appalling slums on the edge of the city. Because there is little work, children are sent into the streets to earn whatever they can.

The streets are crammed with cars and buses and these, together with hundreds of factories, have created an immense pollution problem. The city is often covered by a dark, grey mist. There is also a shortage of water, as Mexico City is not built near a river. Finally, the lake bed on which the city is built has become unstable, partly as a result of earthquakes and tremors. Some of the city's buildings are gradually sinking.

Boys on the street, Mexico City

Tortillas and beans

A family lunch in a restaurant

Many foods with which we are familiar first came from Mexico. Maize has always been the most important crop, and tomatoes, chillies, avocados, beans, turkeys, vanilla flavouring and chocolate also came from this part of the world.

Maize is turned into a *masa*, a dough used for making *tortillas*. Rather like pancakes, *tortillas* can be served with meals or with various fillings. Mexicans like spicy food and sauces, and most dishes contain chillies, peppers, spices and herbs. Chocolate and chilli are used with over 30 other ingredients to make a very rich sauce, or *mole*, which is eaten with chicken or turkey. Black beans called *frijoles* are eaten with many meals and may be served 'refried' as *refritos*.

Strong drink

Maize is also used to make a drink, called *atole*. Water is added to the *tortilla masa* to dilute it, and it is then boiled until it is quite thick. Other local drinks are made from the distilled and fermented juice of agave and cacti plants. One of these, *tequila*, is Mexico's most famous alcoholic drink. The beer-like *pulque*, and *mescal* from Oaxaca are just as strong.

Chocolate and cinnamon

'The greatest chocoholic of all time' is how Montezuma II has been described! The Aztecs drank a great deal of chocolate, believing it to be sacred. They took it with a pinch of cinnamon, a custom that has survived to this day.

Tortillas, *meat, chillies and beans*

> ### Typical dishes
> *tamales* Cornmeal dough filled with meat and chilli sauce, wrapped in corn husks and steamed.
> *tacos* (without chillies) and *enchiladas* (with chillies) Rolled *tortillas* filled with meat, chicken and beans.
> *tostadas* Toasted fried *tortillas* with chicken, beans and lettuce.
> *gorditas* Extra thick *tortillas* with sauce and cheese.
> *guacamole* Avocado dip
> *chiles rellenos* Long green peppers stuffed with cheese or meat, fried and then simmered in a tomato sauce.

Eating out

Mexicans love to eat out, and restaurants and cafés are busy throughout the day. Some are in the attractive, plant-filled patios of old colonial buildings, but at the other extreme there are modern fast-food shops and bars. If you just want a snack, there are *taco* and *tortilla* bars in the busiest city streets, and open-air stalls in the main squares of towns and villages.

Mexican markets

Most cities and towns have large indoor markets, but in rural areas these are usually in the open air. Most of a family's needs can be bought there. Meat, fish, dairy products, including Oaxaca and other local cheeses, household goods, and row upon row of locally grown fresh fruit and vegetables are all on sale. People go to markets not just to buy and sell, but to see friends and have a chat.

The indoor market, Guanajuato

Having fun

Ballgames were being played on special stone courts hundreds of years ago in ancient Mexico. Today you can play almost any modern sport in Mexico. *Fútbol* (soccer) is the most popular. Important matches are played in the Aztec and Olympic stadiums in Mexico City, but all cities, towns and villages have their own teams.

Mexicans take part in many international sporting contests, including tennis, motor racing, hockey, watersports, horse-riding, polo and boxing. For a leisurely day off, families may head for the countryside or the beach, where they take every opportunity to swim, snorkel or simply laze in the sun.

Mexico has over 220 permanent bullrings. The Spanish invaders brought bullfighting to the region. The largest bullring in the world is in Mexico City. It has room for 60 000 spectators. The 'big season' of experienced bullfighters takes place from October to March. The stadium is usually full of spectators.

Another sport inherited from the Europeans is the Basque game of *jai alai*, or *pelota vasca*, played on a 50 metre- (165 foot-) long court with a curved, wicker racket and a hard rubber ball. It is said to be the fastest game in the world.

Sporting events

Mexico has hosted the Olympic Games once, in 1968, and the football World Cup Finals twice, in 1970 and 1986.

The oldest bullring in the Americas is in Mexico City. The first bullfight took place here in the 1520s.

A village rodeo in the Sierra Madre mountains

Bucking broncos

A Mexican rodeo is called '*la charrería*'. The *charros*, or cowboys, show off their skills of roping, tying, riding and branding cattle. These skills were widely used in the old days, before the large cattle ranches were broken up. *Charros* were once sent to fight in the wars as cavalry, because they could easily lasso an enemy. At the *charrería* the cowboys also perform tricks on horseback, and other events include bronco-bucking and bull-riding.

Fiestas

Mexicans love parties and *fiestas*. It is said that you can find a festival somewhere in Mexico every day of the year. People celebrate in style with music, dancing and fireworks. They wear elaborate, brilliantly coloured costumes, often with masks and feathers.

The most important national day commemorates Mexican Independence on September 15, when Father Hidalgo's famous cry '*El Grito de Dolores*' is heard throughout the country at 11am. The most important festival is in honour of the Virgin of Guadalupe, at her shrine in Mexico City in early December.

Dancers at the Virgin of Guadalupe festival

Piñatas

For children, Christmas means piñatas. These are papier-mâché toy animals and figures, which adults fill with toys and sweets. The piñatas are hung high on a rope and childen, blindfolded, have three chances to hit them with a stick to get the contents.

The world of the arts

One of Mexico's most remarkable writers lived in colonial times. She was a seventeenth-century nun called Juana Inés de la Cruz, who wrote poetry and plays. Many Mexican writers and artists take their themes from their rich Native American and Spanish heritage. The best known writer today is Carlos Fuentes. His novels have been translated into many languages. Octavio Paz is the most famous poet. In 1990 he was the first Mexican to receive the Nobel Prize for literature.

The visual arts

For most people, Mexican modern art means the work of the great wall painters, or muralists. In Mexico City and many other towns huge wall paintings can be seen by Diego Rivera (1886-1957), David Alfaro Sigueiros (1898-1974), José Clemente Orozco (1883-1949) and others. Much of their painting shows the history and conflicts of their country, and the hopes expressed by the revolution of 1910. Among the most impressive murals is Rivera's 'History of Mexico' in the National Palace.

Mexico has one of the largest film and television industries in Latin America. International film-makers and writers often use Mexico as a location.

A mural by Diego Rivera, of the Aztec market in Tenochtitlán

A magazine and book stall

Many cowboy films have been made near Durango. The great Spanish film-maker Luis Buñuel settled in Mexico and made a film about the poor of Mexico City, *Los Olvidados* ('The Forgotten Ones').

> ### The press
> Mexico City had the first printing press in the New World. The tradition has been carried on and today Mexico City is one of the most important book-publishing centres in the Spanish-speaking world.

Music and dance

Mexico's most famous classical composer is Carlos Chávez whose works have been heard all over the world. But the musicians most associated with Mexico are *mariachi* bands. Dressed in black and white, with cowboy boots and large *sombreros*, they play sentimental music, mostly on trumpets, violins and guitars, as they stroll through the streets and city squares.

The most spectacular folk dance is the *voladores* or flying pole dance. It is an ancient rain dance of the Totonac people. Four men secured to a 30 metre – 100 foot – high pole by ropes, launch themselves from the top and swing down, head first, circling round the pole until they reach the ground.

Pottery and weavings

Handicrafts are made and sold everywhere in Mexico, and not just for tourists. Oaxaca is well known for black glazed pottery, weavings, basket work, glass, carved wood and leather goods. Elsewhere markets sell brightly coloured pâpier-maché animals and birds, lacquer work, painted ceramics and jewellery.

Silver jewellery on sale in Taxco

Working the land

More than a quarter of Mexico's population is involved in farming. Many are smallholders with plots of land only large enough to feed their families.

If there is any spare produce they sell it at the local market. Their main crop is maize and they usually keep some chickens, pigs or goats. Many people are very poor and few can afford fertilizers or modern machinery.

There are other problems too. The land is too mountainous and the climate too dry. Irrigation is too expensive for all but the larger commercial farms. It has been introduced successfully in the north and northwest, where the main cash crops are cotton and wheat. Coffee, Mexico's chief export crop, and sugar cane are grown in the southern plains. Fruit of every kind is plentiful and grows well along fertile river valleys.

Cattle ranching

In the last century Mexico had vast cattle estates, but today most livestock is raised on small ranches. In the north, despite the dry climate and poor grazing, substantial amounts of meat are produced for sale in Mexico and overseas. New breeds of beef cattle, such as Herefords, are being introduced in this region and production is likely to increase. Cattle are

Farmworkers cutting maize stalks

Fishing in the Gulf of Mexico

also being raised in the south, in areas where the tropical rainforest has been cleared to make way for grazing.

Sardines and shrimps

The fishing industry has become very important since Mexico formed a commercial fishing fleet in the 1960s. Coastal waters in the Gulf of Mexico are rich in shrimps, and many tonnes are exported. But it is the waters around Baja California which are the country's main fishing grounds. The most important catches are tuna, sardines and anchovies, but shark, squid, lobster and other shellfish are also caught. Inland, many villagers make a living from fishing in lakes, using small boats and hand nets.

Forestry

Most of Mexico's tropical forests are in the east and south. They cover about a quarter of the country. They are rich in valuable hardwoods such as American oaks and mahogany, cedar and rosewood.

These are in great demand for the furniture industry. Other valuable trees are the pines and other conifers that grow in the centre of the country. They are cut and used to make wood pulp and paper. However, it is only recently that the trees have been used for timber. The danger is that too much forest may be cut down in the future.

Chewing gum trees

Sapodilla trees are found in the rainforests of Chiapas and the southern Yucatán. Men cut the bark to get *chicle*, a sticky substance used for making chewing gum.

Cutting the bark of a sapodilla tree

Energy and industry

Mexico is very rich in natural resources. Oil was first discovered early this century and by 1984 Mexico had become the world's fourth largest producer. It has huge reserves along the coast of the Gulf of Mexico. Oil, natural gas and coal provide most of the energy that Mexico needs. Power is also generated by hydro-electric plants built on some of Mexico's rivers.

The country also has many precious metals. It is a leading producer of silver, zinc, lead, copper and mercury. Recently large deposits of uranium and gold have also been found.

Mexicans at work

Mexico's immense resources have helped it to become one of the fastest growing industrial countries in the world. Almost half the manufacturing industries are based in Mexico City. Here, factories make and assemble cars, process food and drink, produce electronics equipment, iron and steel and many consumer goods such as washing machines and refrigerators. Outside the capital, Guadalajara and Monterrey are important industrial cities.

Working for dollars

Maquiladores are a new development in Mexican industry. They are factories on the Mexican side of the US border. They are mostly owned by US companies, attracted by the cheap labour force. Mexicans earn their dollars making low-priced electronic goods and television sets for the US market.

A rig in a natural gas field in the Gulf of Mexico

Divers at La Quebrada

Foreign tourists

Tourism is very important to the Mexican economy. Almost seven million tourists visited Mexico in 1990, most of them from the USA and Canada. Few countries can offer the tourist so much. Here are some of the world's most impressive ancient ruins, an amazingly varied landscape, beautiful beaches and opportunities for water sports, a wealth of traditional crafts and wonderful food.

Acapulco on the Pacific coast is the most famous Mexican resort, with its fine beaches, expensive hotels and noisy nightlife. Cancún in the Yucatán, purpose-built for US tourists, now has more hotels per square kilometre than anywhere else in the world. However many Mexicans would say that tourists on package holidays rarely see the real Mexico or meet the local people.

Divers of Acapulco

The most famous of the tourist attractions in Acapulco are the divers at La Quebrada. Young men make the dangerous 12 metre (40 foot) dive over the curving cliff several times a day.

On the move

The great mountain ranges have always made it difficult to build a good road or rail network in Mexico. Air travel has made a great difference, with small aircraft able to land in even the most remote parts of the country.

Mexico City, with almost half of the country's motor vehicles, has a severe traffic problem. An underground railway, the Metro, has been built to ease the congestion. The trains are always very crowded. At rush-hour in some stations, there are separate lanes for women and children to prevent them getting hurt in the crush.

A traffic jam in Mexico City

Modern Mexico

Workers demonstrate against the government

In 1929 the Institutional Revolutionary Party (PRI) was formed, and it has been in government ever since – longer than any other political party in the world. The presidency of Lázaro Cárdenas (1934-40) brought about many of the reforms demanded by the revolution. In 1958 women were allowed to vote for the first time.

For most of these years, Mexico grew more prosperous, but life for the poor remained very hard. Today, many families still earn barely enough for a simple diet of beans, rice and *tortillas*. Many have homes without light, water or sanitation.

During the 1980s and 90s opposition grew to the power of the PRI. There were uprisings in Chiapas in 1994. There were serious problems in the economy. There were social problems too as Mexico's population was increasing faster than in any other major country. In 1988, the PRI candidate, Carlos Salinas de Gortari won the presidential election, but with only a small majority. The PRI won again in 1994, even though their main candidate was assassinated during the campaign. Ernesto Zedillo became president.

Too many people?

Mexico's total population of 88 million people could double in only 29 years time. Half the population is under 20 years old. Today, nearly 30 per cent of the population live in just three cities – Mexico City, Guadalajara and Monterrey.

> ### International debt
> When huge reserves of oil were discovered in the 1970s, the government borrowed vast sums of money from other countries to create new industries. A few years later the world had too much oil, and Mexico could not sell at a good price. As a result it could not pay its debts and many people were out of work.

Northern neighbours

Mexico's relationship with the USA is especially important. Mexico trades more with the rest of North America than it does with all other countries put together. It also sells three times more to the USA than it buys.

But the difference in wealth and power between the two countries has meant that relations are strained. Up to four million Mexicans a year try to cross into the USA illegally, hoping to find better

Waiting to cross the US border

Children playing in Mexico City

working and living conditions. Border patrol guards turn many back.

The movement in the other direction is by tourists. Tijuana claims to be 'the world's most visited city', as 35 million people cross the border from the USA every year.

Free trade

President Salinas tried to open up trade between Mexico and the rest of the world. He encouraged other countries to invest in Mexico. He reduced the country's international debt, cut inflation and signed a treaty with the other countries of North America – the USA and Canada. This agreement allows free trade between the three countries.

The future of Mexico looks bright, provided it remains politically stable and governments ensure that any new prosperity will benefit *all* the people of Mexico.

Fact file

Government

Mexico is a federal republic. Mexico has 31 states as well as the Federal District of Mexico City. Each state has a governor and a Chamber of Deputies elected by the people.

The Mexican head of state is the President, who is elected every six years but cannot serve twice. The President governs with the National Congress. The National Congress is made up of two houses. The Senate has 64 members who are elected every six years. The Chamber of Deputies has 500 members who are elected every three years. Every adult over 18 years of age is obliged to vote.

Flag

The Mexican flag has green, white and red vertical stripes, with the national emblem in the centre of the white stripe. The emblem is made up of a brown eagle holding a snake in its beak, standing on a green cactus, with a wreath of oak and laurel beneath. It is based on an ancient Aztec legend.

National Anthem

The Mexican national anthem is *Mexicanos, al grito de guerra*, which dates back to 1854. Words are by F González Bocanegra and music by Jaime Nunó.

Religion

Mexico has no official religion but 90 per cent of the population are Roman Catholics.

Money

The unit of Mexican currency is the *peso*, which is made up of 100 *centavos*.

Education

Most of the schools in Mexico are run by the government or by the church, and are free. School is divided into primary and secondary levels. All children are expected to attend at primary level which is from the age of 6 to 12. They are not obliged to do the secondary level which starts at the age of 12 and lasts for up to six years.

It is probable that soon the law will be changed so that all children will have to go to school until they are sixteen. About 90 per cent of children now go to primary school and in rural areas children are helped with educational programmes on the radio.

Many schools run evening sessions for people who have missed out on part of their schooling.

Newspapers and broadcasting

Mexico has over 280 daily newspapers and many weekly newspapers.

Mexico's national television network, *Televisa*, is based in Mexico City and there are over 400 stations around the country. There are more than 800 commercial radio stations and over 21 million people own a radio.

Some famous people

Montezuma II (1468-1520) was the Aztec emperor at the time of the Spanish conquest

Miguel Hidalgo (1753-1811) was a priest. In 1810 he led the movement for independence from Spain, and was executed in 1811

Benito Juárez (1806-72), a Zapotec Indian who became president of Mexico on two occasions

José Maria Velasco (1840-1902) was Mexico's greatest landscape artist

José Guadalupe Posada (1851-1913) was an engraver. He often drew skulls and skeletons to make fun of people and events of the time

José Vasconcelos (1882-1959) was the Minister of Education who helped Diego Rivera and other artists who painted murals in public places

Diego Rivera (1886-1957), most famous of the mural painters

Rufino Tamayo (1899-1991) was a Zapotec Indian and one of Mexico's leading artists

Juan O'Gorman (1905-82) was a famous architect and mural painter

Frida Kahlo (1910-54) was the wife of Diego Rivera, and a highly respected artist

Mario Moreno (1911-93) was a well-known actor in Mexico

Carlos Fuentes (1928-) is a famous Mexican writer

Richard 'Pancho' Gonzalez (1928-95) was a successful tennis player

Placido Domingo (1941-) is an opera singer who grew up in Mexico. His first performance was in Mexico City in 1961

Some key events in history

1325: Aztecs founded their capital in Tenochtitlán
1502-1520: Montezuma II ruled the Aztec empire
1519: the Spanish conqueror, Hernán Cortés, reached the Gulf coast
1521: Cortés captured Tenochtitlán
1810: Father Miguel Hidalgo called for independence from Spain
1821: Mexico won its independence from Spain
1822-1823: Mexico was ruled by Emperor Agustín I
1824: Mexico became a federal republic
1834-1847: Antonio López de Santa Anna was President. He was deposed in 1845 and then re-instated in 1846
1848: Treaty of Guadalupe Hidalgo. Mexico lost Texas, California and other lands to the USA
1853-1854: Santa Anna ruled Mexico as a dictator
1857-1864: Benito Juárez was President
1864-1867: Emperor Maximilian I ruled Mexico
1867-1872: Benito Juárez was President of Mexico for the second time. He died in 1872
1876-1911: Porfirio Díaz was president
1910-1917: The Mexican Revolution
1934-1940: Lázaro Cárdenas, as President, made many reforms
1958: Women were given the vote
1985: A major earthquake hit Mexico City
1988: Hurricane Gilbert damaged Cancún and Cozumel island killing about 200 people

Index

Acapulco 6, 27
arts 10-11, 17, 22-23
Aztecs 5, 11, 12, 16, 17, 18, 22, 30, 31

Baja California 9, 25
beaches 5, 8, 20, 27

Cancún 8, 27
Cárdenas, Lázaro 13, 28, 31
Caribbean Sea 5, 8
Chiapas 6, 15, 25, 28
churches 5, 15
climate 7, 24
clothes 14, 15
Cortés, Hernán 12, 31
crafts 15, 16, 23, 27

dance 21, 23
deserts 5, 9, 15
drink 18

earthquakes 16, 17, 31
education 30

families 14, 15
farming 6, 9, 11, 24-25
festivals 14, 15, 21
fishing 10, 25
flag 30
food 18-19, 27, 28
forests 5, 6, 8, 9, 25

government 12, 13, 28, 29, 30
Guadalajara 6, 26, 29
Gulf of Mexico 5, 8, 25, 26

Hidalgo, Miguel 12, 21, 31

industry 26

Juárez, Benito 13, 31

La Paz 9
languages 14, 15

markets 5, 11, 15, 16, 19, 22, 24
Maya 5, 6, 8, 10, 15
mestizos 14, 15

Mexicali 9
Mexico City 5, 6, 7, 13, 14, 16-17, 20, 21, 22, 23, 26, 27, 29, 30, 31
Monterrey 26, 29
Montezuma II 11, 17, 18, 31
mountains 5, 6, 7, 15, 27
music 21, 23

national parks 9
newspapers 30

Oaxaca valley 6, 10, 15
oil 26, 29
Olmecs 10

plains 5, 6, 24
population 6, 16, 17, 28-29
Puebla 6
pyramids 5, 8, 11

religion 12, 15, 30
Río Bravo 5
Rivera, Diego 22, 31
rodeos 21

Santa Anna, López de 12-13, 31
Spanish conquest 5, 11, 12, 20, 31
sport 8, 20, 27

television 30
temples 5, 10-11
Tenochtitlán 11, 16, 17, 22, 31
Tijuana 9, 29
Toltecs 5, 11
tourism 5, 6, 8, 27, 29

United States of America 5, 6, 13, 26, 27, 29

Veracruz 8
Villa, Pancho 13
volcanoes 5, 7

wildlife 9

Yucatán 8, 10, 15, 25, 27

Zapata, Emiliano 13
Zapotecs 10, 13, 15, 31